# MAY 4TH VOICES

# MAY 4TH VOICES

# KENT STATE, 1970

**WITHDRAWN**

*A Play*

*David Hassler*

THE KENT STATE UNIVERSITY PRESS   KENT, OHIO

Ohio Arts Council
A STATE AGENCY
THAT SUPPORTS PUBLIC
PROGRAMS IN THE ARTS

The voice of the Narrator is excerpted from Maj Ragain's prose poem, "May 4, 1970 / A Memory," from *A Hungry Ghost Surrenders His Tacklebox,* published by Pavement Saw Press in 2006, and used here by permission of the poet and publisher.

**TO KENT STATE STUDENTS—**

*past, present, and future.*

# CONTENTS

# FOREWORD

*Tom Hayden*

"A small encampment of listeners bending to the hard lessons" is the way a student discussion of Vietnam is described in David Hassler's *May 4th Voices*. This is not a play in the conventional sense, but bursts of live feelings recorded by the Kent State Shootings Oral History Project and woven together now to reenact the trauma of those days. One must hope that this reenactment of the trauma will touch audiences today so deeply that they become "encampments bending to hear hard lessons" once again.

Is it absurd to think so? There always are creative minorities hungry at the table of memory, and I have great faith in the method employed here, because it is about direct participation in the reenactment as spoken word.

There is no greater method of teaching history than encouraging later generations to inhabit the lives of those who came before. When students are required to become the characters here—someone shot on the way to class, a tense National Guardsman, or an adult Kent resident who believes the protestors should be crushed—something happens to them. They must become immersed in the spoken lines of a real person; they must study the context of long ago; they must internalize the emotions and dynamics of the time. History is not delivered to them; it is relived by them. In the best case, the audience relives the experience too. Participatory history is powerful pedagogy.

I have seen the power of this kind of performance in the reenactments of two other dramas of the period, the Chicago Conspiracy Trial, revolving around the protests at the August 1968 Democratic Convention, and the Trial of the Catonsville Nine for the theft and burning of draft files at Catonsville, Maryland, just three months earlier. Plays and films based on the transcripts of these two trials, which occurred at the same time as the events at Kent State and Jackson State, drew vast audiences in the decades to come. The most interesting of these in my experience was a live reenactment by students at an Ohio university a few years ago, before an audience of five hundred for five nights. The students were fully engaged in the forty or so roles they performed in the Chicago trial—from the defendants to the U.S. marshals—and the audience of students and townspeople was fully engaged too. This was a relived history for young people who knew nothing about their parents' generation, and a way to emerge from the silence of a traumatic past for the older audience.

I believe David Hassler is correct in observing that the performance of *May 4th Voices* will enable many people in Ohio—and beyond—to recover memories of a shattering time in our country's life, a time that one of the "voices" remembers as when "the country came as close to a civil war between generations as you'd probably ever want to see."

A time when male students defined themselves as numbers on a draft board list: "By lunch time, when you met another guy on campus, you wouldn't ask what their number was, you wouldn't even say hello, you'd just greet each other by saying, '263,' and the other guy would say, '48,' and then you'd start your conversation from there. . . . It was your ID."

A time when a women student thought: "I felt so grateful I was not a guy. So grateful that I had no brothers."

A time when a young National Guard member had to worry that "if you got five 'unsats,' five unsatisfactories, you were sent to active duty."

A time when, to engage their apathetic fellows, students put out a leaflet announcing their plan to napalm a dog. "So about three or four hundred students showed up in front of the Hub, the old student union, to stop us from napalming this dog."

A time when students saw that the facades of banks were not built of marble but of chicken wire and plaster, emptiness behind the edifice. "I never realized these pillars could be anything but solid. It felt like my whole town was just a stage set—all surface and fragile."

And, ultimately, a time when destiny arrived as a rent veil.

"After the shooting, it got totally quiet. I just heard air hissing out of a tire—that sound, *bsssshhhoouu.* Time had totally stopped. Now, subsequently, I've figured out what it was. When people die violently, a veil is rent and you're thrust into the next plane. And anyone who's tuned to the event feels this rush from a door opening. So the veil is rent, torn away. And any kind of evil thoughts that are there from humanity's beginning are available at this moment. And depending on how sensitive you are, you can hear it, feel it, or see it."

There is little scripted here, just raw words that have waited for hearts and open minds since 1970. Raw words floating toward "encampments bending to listen to hard lessons," wherever they might gather.

The sixties experience is entering the realm of memory, to be discarded, distorted, demonized—or discovered, as if for the first time, and dramatized in the legacy of social movements.

America owes it to our children that these voices live.

# ACKNOWLEDGMENTS

The idea for *May 4th Voices* grew out of many conversations and was developed through the creative and collaborative involvement of many people. The play was originally written and performed as part of a larger, multifaceted community arts project in honor of the 40th Commemoration of the May 4th tragedy. Conceived with Laura Davis, professor of English and faculty coordinator for May 4th initiatives; Anderson Turner, director of the Kent State School of Art Galleries; and the Wick Poetry Center, with funding from the Ohio Humanities Council, this project involved an interactive art installation in downtown Kent, a community story quilt, and writing workshops with area veterans, schoolchildren, and community members around the themes of peace and reconciliation.

I want to thank the Wick Poetry Center staff, Nicole Robinson, Jessica Jewell, and Rachelle Chavez; and our many student interns and fellows, who have developed and implemented the larger, community implications of this project; and also the Wick family, who continue to support the programming of the Wick Poetry Center.

I thank Laura Davis, who first told me about the digital oral history archives in 2009 and encouraged me to delve into them. These archives would not exist were it not for the vision and energy of Sandra Perlman Halem, who began the Kent State Shootings Oral History Project in 1990. I am grateful for Sandy's foresight and for her own creative work that inspired this play.

I am grateful to Steve Paschen, Kent State University archivist, who now maintains this remarkable ongoing oral history project, which is housed in Kent State University Libraries' Department of Special Collections and Archives.

I am very grateful to Katherine Burke, who developed a Devising Theatre class in 2010 around the May 4th shootings and oral history and originally staged the play with Kent State undergraduate students and community members. Katherine's expertise was essential in editing, revising, and, finally, shaping the script for the stage. In addition to teaching, directing, and script development, she served as the stage manager, box office manager, the props, costume, lighting, sound, and the you-name-it manager for just about every other detail. I am also grateful for my longtime friend and collaborator, Hal Walker, who created the music for the first production. I also appreciate Cynthia Stillings, Director of the KSU School of Theatre and Dance, who supported this project from the beginning.

As I mention in my introduction, the script would not have come together in a cohesive whole without the voice of Maj Ragain as the narrator. I am grateful to Maj, my friend and mentor, who reminded me of his four-page prose poem, "May 4, 1970 / A Memory," which became the voice of the narrator threaded throughout the play.

I am also grateful for the insightful comments of Alice Cone, Laura Kepley, Jeff St. Clair, and Jeff Hooper, who read earlier versions of the play; for Tom Hatch, John Morris, and Heidi Summerlin, who developed the idea of the teacher's guide along with many Kent Roosevelt High School teachers; and for the encouragement and support of Patrick Coy, Patrick Chura, Bob Balla, Judith Royer, Doris Baizley, and Tom Hayden.

A big thanks to Ken Bindas, who has championed this project at Kent State University, creating a Teacher's Summer Institute and coproducing a filmed version of the play. And a very big thanks to Mathias Peralta and his talented film crew: Robert Makar, Chris Young, Jorge Delarosa, Dylan Lusk, Ruth Turner, and David Burkhart.

I thank The Kent State University Press and its staff for their vision and willingness to publish this play and the accompanying teacher's guide and film, in particular the acquiring editor and Press director, Will Underwood.

My wife, Lynn Gregor, is always my first reader and my most honest critic. I appreciate her love and support.

I am deeply grateful to the three different casts who have staged this play during the last two years. These passionate Kent State undergraduate students and community members have opened their hearts and minds to give voice to the experience of Kent State students and of our community of over forty years ago. Their courage and honesty to engage and embody these voices remains for me a great source of inspiration and hope.

And finally, I am grateful to all the people who have contributed their stories to the ongoing oral history project. I hope this play honors the truth and integrity of their voices.

# INTRODUCTION

On May 4, 1970, four students were killed and nine injured on the campus of Kent State University by the Ohio National Guard during a Vietnam War protest. Nearly forty years later, I began work on a play, based on the ongoing Kent State Shootings Oral History Project, for the 40th Commemoration of the May 4th tragedy. This remarkable collection of oral histories, begun in 1990 by Sandra Perlman Halem and now housed in the Kent State University Libraries' Department of Special Collections and Archives, includes over 110 interviews that document first-person narratives and personal reactions to the events of May 4, 1970. When I first read through these transcripts and listened to the audio, I was struck by the common thread that ran through them all. Nearly every interviewee—whether they were a student, Kent resident, faculty, or guardsman—expressed a similar feeling of fear and confusion and admitted that they had not spoken about their memories and experiences of that event until their interview. They had silenced themselves. These interviews sounded like a kind of "coming out"—each person giving voice for the first time to what had been hidden inside them.

One of the chief hallmarks of trauma is silencing, not just personally but also collectively, within communities and within a larger society. The emerging field of trauma studies has uncovered two essential experiences all trauma victims must undertake to recover from their ordeal: creative self-expression and membership in community. Trauma survivors must be allowed to tell the truth about their experiences, and members of the sufferer's community must be encouraged to listen, to remember, and to repeat the story to others. This is what clinical psychiatrist Dr. Jonathan Shay calls the "process of communalizing" trauma; and this is the place where artists and the arts have played a role since the beginning of time.

My interest in this material is quite personal. I grew up in Kent and on May 4, 1970, was in first grade. I was sent home from Longcoy Elementary School because of bomb threats and remember watching

1

National Guardsmen and armed vehicles move through my small college town. I saw an army helicopter land in the neighborhood where we played pickup games of baseball and freeze tag. Yet no adults explained these events to us children. My memories of May 4th are those of a sheltered young child. And throughout my public education in Kent, the May 4th tragedy was rarely mentioned or taught. But in reading through the oral history archives, and in weaving these voices together and shaping the play, I had the sense that the voices of student protestors, guardsmen, faculty, and residents were, for the first time, listening and speaking to each other—having a conversation they could not have had then.

The play is composed entirely of these excerpts, except for the voice of the narrator. Near the end of the scripting process, my poet friend and mentor Maj Ragain, who was a graduate student on campus that day and now teaches creative writing at Kent State, reminded me of his four-page prose poem, "May 4, 1970 / A Memory." As I reread his poem, I saw, uncannily, how large verbatim excerpts could fit perfectly as the voice of the narrator threaded throughout the script, observing and commenting on the dramatic events, not unlike the role of the Stage Manager in Thornton Wilder's *Our Town*. The voice of Maj's poem, as narrator, was what the play needed to give a larger context and perspective to the fragmented narratives and stories.

After working for nine months with these transcripts, I handed the script to Katherine Burke, an instructor in the theatre department at Kent State. She was teaching a special semester-long three-credit Devising Theatre class called "May 4th, Past, Present." Thirteen students had enrolled in the class, each with varying degrees of acting experience. The students spent the first half of the semester devising scenes and movement to explore their own responses to the voices in the oral history archive. Then in the second half of the semester they were given the early draft of the play and began to work on staging and the text itself. In staging the play with her students, Katherine broke up many of the monologue sequences further, to intercut the voices for dramatic effect and pacing.

The original production of the play on May 2, 2010, was performed with scripts in hand in a reader's theatre style with minimal props and staging. Maj agreed to perform his own lines as the narrator, and Katherine's students—with great passion, seriousness, and, indeed, some humor—brought to life the voices from a generation ago. In the final scene, "Legacy," we had arranged for members of our own community—young and old—seated in the audience to step up to the stage and deliver a line or brief monologue, to speak a voice not their own. Nearly five hundred people attended the performance, and over half of them stayed for an open audience conversation with the cast afterwards.

Kent State carries the symbolic wound of the Vietnam War and the protest movement in this country, along with the tragedy ten days later at Jackson State in which two African American students were killed and twelve others wounded in a similar antiwar protest. Engaging any community in the healing process of creating art and providing venues for the public to witness has the power to heal. If, as the fourteenth-century Persian poet Rumi says, "the medicine is in the wound," then *May 4th Voices* is an attempt to speak directly from the wound of Kent State and this cultural period, to move beyond a polarizing silence, and to create a space—like the ritual space of theatre—in which we might listen and respond to each other.

*David Hassler, November 2012*

# PRODUCTION NOTES

*May 4th Voices* was first performed at Kent State University on May 2, 2010, directed by Katherine Burke, for the 40th annual May 4th Commemoration. The original cast was comprised of Maj Ragain as narrator and thirteen students who were enrolled in a semester-long Devising Theatre class taught by Katherine Burke in the Kent State School of Theatre and Dance.

Subsequent productions, directed by Katherine Burke, were featured at Case Western Reserve University's International Peace and War Conference in October 2010 and the Oral History Association's International Conference in October 2012.

All the text in the script has been edited and arranged based on the Kent State Shootings Oral History Project, housed in Kent State University Libraries' Department of Special Collections and Archives, except for the voice of the narrator, which is excerpted from Maj Ragain's prose poem, "May 4, 1970 / A Memory," from *A Hungry Ghost Surrenders His Tacklebox,* published by Pavement Saw Press in 2006, and used here by permission.

## CASTING

Because the Devising Theatre class had only thirteen members (six males, seven females), we manipulated the script for the original production to fit exactly that many people—plus one narrator. Future productions, however, may use as many actors as are available. The only requirement is that the actors portray these voices with the truthfulness and dignity they deserve. Female actors may play male characters, and male actors may play female characters. A variety of ages are represented in the script, but there is no need to cast age-appropriate actors. On the contrary, there is a certain poignancy to a young actor speaking the words of an older voice, and vice versa.

## SET AND COSTUMES

Since we had a very small budget in the spring of 2010, the original performance used wooden chairs and sheer white fabric. The lack of financing had initially seemed like an obstacle, but it turned out to be a blessing because the stark neutrality of the set forced us to be imaginative. The actors arranged the chairs to form a car (which was "rocked" by draping fabric over the people and pulling it back and forth), hills, walls, podiums, interrogation rooms, and more. The fabric was used as blankets, rivers, paths, hair, clothes, and in symbolic ways as well. The actors wore neutral clothing, so they could easily represent a variety of characters. We had discussed the possibility of using imagery and projections, but we decided against it, as May 4th imagery is so iconic and charged with emotion; we wanted the audience to focus on the words. I encourage you to use as simple a set as possible and to play with the many ways you can arrange bodies, tables, chairs, stools, fabric, rope, or whatever you have lying around.

## MUSIC AND SOUND

We found it particularly effective to use music and sound effects to make transitions from one scene to the next, to punctuate or intensify a moment, and to establish atmosphere and context. In the original performance, we were fortunate to have live music and sound effects provided by Kent musician and resident Hal Walker, who played an assortment of familiar and strange instruments to help create the world of the play. If you have live music available, if your actors are able to play instruments, or if you have a sound designer, sound and music can play an important role in the performance.

# SCENES AND CHARACTERS

**SCENE ONE:**
**THE LOTTERY**
*Context of the sixties and
Vietnam War*
    Narrator
    4 Male Students
    2 Female Students
    2 Faculty Members
    2 Guardsmen
    2 Kent Residents
    1 High School Teacher

**SCENE TWO:**
**SOMETHING DRASTIC**
*Thursday and Friday*
    Narrator
    2 Male Students
    2 Female Students

**SCENE THREE:**
**THE WHOLE TOWN IS
BURNING**
*Saturday and Sunday*
    1 Male Student
    3 Female Students
    1 Mother
    4 Guardsmen
    2 Young Kent Residents
    1 Old Lady

**SCENE FOUR:**
**THE RALLY**
*Monday leading up*
    Narrator
    3 Male Students

**SCENE FIVE:**
**A VEIL IS RENT**
*The shootings*
    4 Male Students
    4 Female Students
    2 Guardsmen

**SCENE SIX:**
**INTENSIVE CARE**
*Later that day*
    2 Male Students
    1 Female Student
    1 Young Kent Resident
    1 Guardsman
    1 Jr. High School Student
    1 High School Student

**SCENE SEVEN:**
**REACTIONARY**
*Throughout that summer*
    Narrator
    3 Male Students
    2 Female Students
    1 Faculty Member
    1 BBC Producer
    2 Kent Residents
    1 Guardsman
    1 Employer
    1 Brother
    1 Relative

**SCENE EIGHT:**
**GETTING IN THE WAY**
**OF BULLETS**
*Grand Jury and FBI*
*investigation*
    2 Male Students
    1 Female Student
    1 Faculty Member

    1 Mom
    3 FBI Agents
    2 Police Officers
    1 Prosecutor
    1 Sheriff
    1 Attorney General
    1 BBC Producer
    2 Kent Residents
    1 Guardsman

**SCENE NINE:**
**VIGIL**
*Legacy of trauma*
    Narrator
    5 Male Students
    5 Female Students
    1 Guardsman
    2 Alumni

# SCENE ONE: THE LOTTERY

Narrator
4 Male Students
2 Female Students
2 Faculty Members
2 Guardsmen
2 Kent Residents
1 High School Teacher
1 Mother

**NARRATOR**

I first came to Kent on a July morning, 1969. I was twenty-nine years old, having driven all night from Illinois, hungover, raw, leaving the carnival undertow of my youth, hot dreams, and crazy love. I first saw the town from Route 59, the cluster of buildings catching the sun. I remember thinking it looked like the photographs of an Italian town reared up in the sky. Years later, when I got to Italy, some of the towns looked, from a distance, like Kent. I was glad to find a river and railroad tracks, a brick train station, water, and steel joining this to that. The overpass, Haymaker Parkway, was still on the drawing boards. I entered Kent over the old Main Street bridge and right onto Water Street. Always find a water street. I settled into the Allerton apartments at eighty bucks a month and began life as a graduate student. I wasn't much good at it, spent too much time at Walter's bar on Water Street, gave my heart away every full moon, and took incompletes in my classes. By then, the Vietnam Veterans Against the War had organized in Kent. I remember them stopping traffic on Main Street, in front of Captain Brady's Café, a hundred or more of them, marching rag tag, bearded, silent, some amputees, a couple of men rolling wheelchairs, Coxie's army come home. Later that day, the vets held a teach-in at Fred Fuller Park, under the big trees, a small encampment of listeners bending to the hard lessons.

**MALE STUDENT 1**

The first draft lottery was December 1st, 1969. It's one of those dates I'll never forget.

**MALE STUDENT 2**

If you didn't go through those times it's hard to understand what was going through people's heads . . .

**MALE STUDENT 1**

I had a high number—263 or something. And the day after, on campus, with the first few guys you would meet, you would ask, "What was your number last night?" And somebody would say, "Oh, mine was 300-something." And somebody else would say, "3." And you knew he was drafted.

**MALE STUDENT 2**

. . . because actually, only a couple of years ago I finally put my draft card away. I carried it from the time I was eighteen until my mid-fifties.

**MALE STUDENT 1**

By lunch time, when you met another guy on campus, you wouldn't ask what their number was, you wouldn't even say hello, you'd just greet each other by saying, "263," and the other guy would say, "48," and then you'd start your conversation from there.

**MALE STUDENT 2**

It wasn't supposed to be for identification, but you couldn't go anywhere if you were a male and over 18, without it—it was your ID.

**FEMALE STUDENT 1**

I loved my college years but at the same time I remember the anxiety I suffered.

**MALE STUDENT 1**

That was all that was being discussed that day.

**FEMALE STUDENT 2**

The constant feelings of stress, the heartbeat rate being elevated. Starting in 1967 and '68 particularly, when Martin Luther King Jr. was shot, and then Robert Kennedy right in front of our eyes on television. And my friends, of course, going off to Vietnam. There were friends of mine that came back to my hometown that were never the same.

**MALE STUDENT 3**

Kent was my hometown. I grew up here. I started at the university in 1963, but I didn't do so well, so I joined the service.

**GUARDSMAN 1**

I was kind of a procrastinator.

**MALE STUDENT 3**

A few years later, I found myself off the coast of Vietnam, and realized this war was wrong. So I told my division officer I would not pull the trigger if it were to come to that. This was near the end of my enlistment and I returned to Kent and began school as an antiwar Vietnam veteran.

**GUARDSMAN 1**

I didn't do what many people were doing at the time: either going into college, or joining the National Guard in order to avoid the draft. I hadn't done either and really felt that getting drafted was imminent.

**MALE STUDENT 3**

I marched on Main Street and spoke at the teach-ins.

**GUARDSMAN 1**

I remember my mother called me one day at work and said,

**MOTHER**

"A registered letter came for you, and you can pick it up at the post office. We didn't get it in time from the mailman."

**GUARDSMAN 1**

So that afternoon I called the National Guard and they told me there were one or two openings and there were four people about to interview for them. They told me I could come right down, and if I passed all of their tests, they could swear me in right there. So I went down, passed all of the requirements, and was sworn in. The next day I went to the post office and discovered it was a notice from my insurance company saying I had money coming back to me, because I'd just changed my automobile insurance. It wasn't a draft notice. So this explains why I was in the National Guard. I was not really a serious type of soldier. I didn't feel particularly authoritative or powerful. I just happened to be there, same reason a lot of the kids were in school—to avoid the war.

**GUARDSMAN 2**

You have to realize if you were in the National Guard at that time, if you got five "unsats," five unsatisfactories, you were sent to active duty.

**MALE STUDENT 2**

We all faced that fear of going to Vietnam.

**GUARDSMAN 2**

If your hair was long, if you were out of uniform, if you were late for a drill, you got an unsatisfactory.

**MALE STUDENT 2**

It was the same fear, as if you went to a doctor and he said, "You have cancer."

**GUARDSMAN 2**

You could get four unsatisfactories in a weekend, because a drill was split into four different things. You didn't want to get that golden fifth one 'cause you were outta here, and then you were in active duty.

**MALE STUDENT 2**

It was that same choking fear. And only the men had it. Because we were the only ones that were going.

**GUARDSMAN 2**

They didn't have to send us down for another eight, ten, twelve weeks of training.

**MALE STUDENT 2**

They were only taking the 18-, 19-, 20-year-olds. They weren't taking 30-year-olds. They weren't taking 15-year-olds. It was us!

**GUARDSMAN 2**

It was on a plane and you were over there. Don't think that you weren't threatened with that—you knew that was the sword.

**MALE STUDENT 2**

And without any counseling, without any kind of softening of the blow.

**RESIDENT 1**

I had a drugstore in downtown Kent, and I was hard to argue with in those days—I thought I knew it all. I could sympathize with the young kids because I still thought I was a young kid, but I could identify with government, too. I think the majority of the businessmen were against the war. They'd given it a chance, you know. But I had better communication with the students, because in the drugstore you get to meet everybody, and I'd rather talk to people than fill prescriptions. It was more interesting. I used to argue politics with everybody who came along. One guy would say,

**RESIDENT 2**

"Are you a Democrat?"

**RESIDENT 1**

"Who said that?"

**RESIDENT 3**

"Well, are you a Republican?"

**RESIDENT 1**

"No, I'm just at odds with your position and we're gonna see who wins the argument." But I wore a black armband during that time, and I lost a bunch of customers.

**MALE STUDENT 2**

I was at the Venice Café one time when someone tried to burn a cigarette hole in my coat.

**RESIDENT 4**

"You think you're better than I am, because you go to school up on the hill."

**MALE STUDENT 2**

"No, I don't." But there was a great deal of jealousy and distrust of students. After all, we had an easy life. All we did was party and get laid and we didn't have to work too hard, we didn't have to go to Vietnam.

**FACULTY MEMBER 1**

The Biology Department was very conservative, very right wing, when I joined it. In fact, when I interviewed for the job, in 1967, I was clean-shaven, and was hired. And I showed up in September with a mustache. And you should have seen the looks. I mean, if they could have revoked the contract, I think they would have.

**BLACK STUDENT 1**

Out of around twenty thousand students there were probably only about a thousand black students on the campus. We had our own personal concerns that we were dealing with that white students weren't really concerned with, like trying to get more black teachers on the campus and starting a Black Studies program. These were our primary concerns at the time. A lot of minorities—blacks and Hispanics—had volunteered for the military. Even I had volunteered for the Marines before coming to Kent State. The armed forces was a job opportunity for a lot of blacks. But after Martin Luther King began to speak out, we all became aware that something was wrong with this war.

**FEMALE STUDENT 2**

I think the country came as close to a civil war between generations as you'd probably ever want to see. Because you had old versus young; you had fathers against sons; you had generation against generation. You can call it what you want. But Kent State brought to a boiling point the feelings on both sides.

**FACULTY MEMBER 2**

A lot of professors my age didn't start out radicals, at all.

**MALE STUDENT 2**

So, I was a campus radical in '69.

**FACULTY MEMBER 2**

We started out wondering what was going on.

**MALE STUDENT 2**

But I wasn't a long-haired campus radical and I wasn't as radical as some people.

**FACULTY MEMBER 2**

What the hell are we doing in Vietnam? We were very worried about the implications of getting mired down in something like that. Particularly because we had been brought up to believe that the U.S. had never lost a war and had never been the aggressor. And it was very clear that was never the truth in the first place.

**MALE STUDENT 2**

I think Wordsworth once said about the French Revolution, but it could be said about being young at Kent State, "Bliss it was to be alive, but to be young was very heaven."

**FACULTY MEMBER 2**

What are we trying to accomplish over there? Why are we doing this? And what are we doing to ourselves in the bargain?

**MALE STUDENT 2**

It was a pretty heady experience being twenty, twenty-one, twenty-two years old on the campus of Kent State.

**MALE STUDENT 3**

The day after my twenty-first birthday I led a demonstration in which we threatened to napalm a dog. We were really young people who were out to change the world and take on this incredible responsibility—that, obviously, the older generation had absolved themselves of. I wore a suit and tie just to throw people off—you know, so we didn't look "radical." We had passed out flyers the previous day saying, "For your edification and amusement we're gonna napalm a dog on April 22nd, blah blah blah."

So about three or four hundred students showed up to stop us from napalming this dog in front of the Hub, the old student union. I explained what napalm was, and tried to be as dispassionate and scientific about it as I could. I told the crowd that the U.S. government had developed it at the end of World War II and that it was such a powerful weapon in Vietnam that it could burn people alive. I'll never forget the picture of the three little Vietnamese children running down the road in 1972, with napalm burning on their backs. If I remember nothing else about Vietnam, that would be the picture that seared my mind, and of course, seared those children's bodies beyond belief.

So I said to the crowd, "How many of you people here have come to stop me from napalming this dog?" They all shook their fists and growled. Then I said, "How many of you people are willing to take action to stop me from napalming this dog?" And they shook their fists and growled. I said, "Good for you. You've done the right thing. You've come to stop me from doing a very immoral act. However, your government isn't doing it to just a dog; it's doing it to thousands of people. Just because they live far away, doesn't make it any less immoral. Well there was a deadly silence in the crowd.

And it seemed like you could hear the anguished screams of the Vietnamese halfway around the world. Now, of course, there was never any napalm, or never any dog. And yet, one of the newspapers reported that they took the dog out of my hands. This is how vivid people's imaginations are. It was amazing how people turned out to save a dog.

## FEMALE STUDENT 2

There was a commotion in front of the Music and Speech building. Some members of the Students for a Democratic Society were blocking the doors to the building, because there was a meeting going on over suspensions of students for something or other. And I saw these great big, burly, football-type guys beating the living hell out of both guys and girls who were there demonstrating. And after they got through beating these people up they just stood there and sang "The Star-Spangled Banner." I didn't sing "The Star-Spangled Banner" for about the next ten years. It was my way of protesting that.

## HIGH SCHOOL TEACHER

I had a good rapport with the kids at the high school, because I was young, in my second year of teaching. I was standing outside the atrium doors during lunch hour, when a small crowd of students started to gather. A young man named Paul, who wanted to bring a kind of activism to our school, was talking about the anti-war movement and why people should join in, why the Vietnam War was immoral and so forth. And gradually a different group shifted up to the front. These were the kids whose fathers or brothers were over in Vietnam and they were pretty upset by the things

Paul was saying. They had grim looks. So I moved closer to Paul and stood next to him. And they started to pick up these little tiny gravel stones and bounce them, one by one, off Paul's chest. They weren't throwing them hard, but just tossing them—*ping, ping*. And slowly moving closer. There were maybe ten of them, and these were some big boys, many of them played football and were good kids. I mean they weren't, otherwise, violent kids. But you could see the rage coming over them. Paul just kept on talking. I was the only teacher around, and the only thing I could think to do if they rushed him, was to step in front. There was not much else I could do. I thought, "My God, what's going to happen? They might really go at it, and it may be more than just a fight." And then, suddenly the bell rang.

The whole thing just went "poof," like a balloon collapsing. They all just stopped and went to class. Even Paul stopped speaking. I thought, "Thank God for Pavlov!" They were conditioned to the bell. And hearing the bell they simply stopped and went to class.

I know I earned my pay that day.

# SCENE TWO: SOMETHING DRASTIC

Narrator
2 Male Students
2 Female Students

**NARRATOR**

May 1, 1970. I was downtown in Walter's bar, drinking Rolling Rock and riding a warm spring Ohio night. Nixon had escalated the Vietnam War with the bombing of Cambodia. We all felt betrayed. Around eleven o'clock, after an NBA finals game on TV, the bars swelled over into the street, blocking traffic. Someone dumped a trash container and lit a bonfire on the centerline, then another. The horses of instruction were in the barn. The tigers of wrath were teaching us their wisdom. It was crazy springtime in a country still young, blood surge, hot youth, a protest against every tight bunghole, against every official hand turning the screws on freedom. It was "One, two, three, four, we don't want your fucking war," just like they told you. Only louder. And everybody meant it.

**FEMALE STUDENT 1**

There was a spontaneous party at Glenmorris Apartments. It was a beautiful warm day and people came outside.

**MALE STUDENT 1**

We were in Moulton Hall watching Nixon on TV when our RA counselor announced to us that anyone who didn't have the proper grades, with a 1A classification, would be gone in three weeks to Vietnam.

**FEMALE STUDENT 1**

Passions were running high, fueled by the good weather.

**MALE STUDENT 1**

Well, after Woodstock and all that we went through in the late '60s, this was just not going to work.

**FEMALE STUDENT 1**

We all came out and passed around jugs of wine, and the boys were saying, "What the hell, we're all going to be cannon fodder here."

**MALE STUDENT 1**

My definite feeling was that we're not going and something drastic had to be done.

**FEMALE STUDENT 1**

I felt so grateful I was not a guy. So grateful that I had no brothers.

**MALE STUDENT 2**

My girlfriend and I walked past the ROTC building and we both stopped in mid-step and looked at each other. I said, "You felt that too, huh?" And she said, "Yeah." And it was just this strange cold feeling that wasn't like a physical cold. I can't forget that. We were right beside the building that within twenty-four hours would be burned.

**FEMALE STUDENT 2**

From my perspective it was drinkin' beer and lookin' for guys. I mean that was what it was about. It had been a really long, cold, dark winter, and that weekend was the first weekend of real spring that year. So people were down in the bars, down on Water Street, and were just in one of those youthful, hormonal party places. I was there with a girlfriend. We had decided we were goin' downtown to find her a boyfriend—she'd been lonely too long. But when the streets were blocked off, some people began to throw rocks and break windows. I wasn't in favor of the war, but I didn't see why the people who owned the shoe store and the butchers had anything to do with the cause of the war.

I saw an elderly couple in their car—the light had turned red, and they were stopped in the traffic surrounded by students. And some guys started to rock the car. And the couple was scared, they locked their doors and rolled up their windows. I think people were kind of feeling their oats.

But it went from there.

# SCENE THREE:
# THE WHOLE TOWN IS BURNING

1 Male Student
3 Female Students
1 Mother
4 Guardsmen
2 Young Kent Residents
1 Old Lady

**YOUNG RESIDENT 1**

My exposure to the university was really limited. My sister had gone there, but it was on the other side of town. So Kent, to me, was my school and friends, and the university was what broke the windows on my dad's store.

**YOUNG RESIDENT 2**

I went downtown on Saturday morning to see what had happened, and I walked over to the City Bank on Water Street. I had always looked at its big pillars and believed they were made out of stone, like marble. But they had been gouged and I saw they were just chicken wire and plaster. I never realized these pillars could be anything but solid. It felt like my whole town was just a stage set—all surface and fragile.

**MALE STUDENT 1**

Saturday evening a number of us walked over to the Commons; people were just milling around. There was nothing organized. One student walked up to the old ROTC building and broke out the glass, took his lighter, and started lighting the curtains.

**GUARDSMAN 1**

As we approached campus from Route 76, we had the top down on the jeep, and you could see the glow of the fire from the ROTC building.

**MALE STUDENT 1**

Then I saw a couple others break some more glass, and the amazing thing I noticed was that there were police officers at the top of the hill by the student union. They were just sitting there, watching.

**GUARDSMAN 1**

My first thought was, "My God, the whole town is burning." It was literally an orange glow in the sky.

**YOUNG RESIDENT 1**

I was seven years old, and I lived on Willow Street. I remember the helicopters at night, and my dad driving me downtown to the businesses, and seeing all the windows smashed out in all the buildings.

**YOUNG RESIDENT 2**

A helicopter for Governor Rhodes landed on our playground at the University School. It was both exciting and frightening.

**YOUNG RESIDENT 1**

I really didn't know much about what was going on, but I still saw it. And the one thing that sticks out in my mind is the tanks on my playground, and the soldiers sleeping in the gymnasium. And how the tanks bumped into our jungle gym and made it crooked.

**YOUNG RESIDENT 2**

I was torn between being a child and being an adult—being afraid and picking up on my parents' fears, and wanting to be up there with the big kids.

**YOUNG RESIDENT 1**

That's the one thing that sticks out in my mind.

**GUARDSMAN 1**

We were put up in an elementary school gymnasium and sleeping on the floor. At best they were horrible conditions because the lights were on and we constantly had troops coming and going, and we got little, if any, sleep. Sunday morning, I called my fiancée and said, "I want a real meal. Can you bring me some real food?" She said, "Sure." So I waited outside to flag her down. Well, there I was in uniform, with a helmet and an M-1, waiting on Mogadore Road. And when I spotted her coming down Cherry Street, I waved and three or four cars pulled over. People got out of their cars and put their hands up. I said, "No, no," and just motioned everybody to go on through. It was eight or nine o'clock in the morning, and one couple said, "We're just goin' to church." And then it hit me that here was a town under siege, just like we'd seen in the movies our whole life, and I thought, "My God, here I am, a 20-some-year-old kid with a gun, and people are pulling off the streets for me."

**YOUNG RESIDENT 2**

When we got home from Mass, we turned on the radio in the living room, and we all sat and listened to Governor Rhodes make his statements. He was in town with the mayor. I don't remember his exact words, but it was something like, "No Goddamn students are gonna close down a campus under my watch in my state" kind of a thing. He may have even said, "hippie-students." This was all kind of crazy to me.

**GUARDSMAN 2**

We were actually told that we were going to stop the crowd from going downtown. I knew some of the businessmen in town, and to this day I think it's just as well because, believe me, the businessmen were better armed than we were. There were people sitting on rooftops, and had those students moved on downtown to trash it again, there would have been gunfire. It was that simple. It was like saving someone from themselves.

**FEMALE STUDENT 1**

My mother called me on Sunday and said . . .

**MOTHER**

"You need to come home."

**FEMALE STUDENT 1**
"Why?"

**MOTHER**
"Well, you've got people with guns on your campus. You need to come home."

**FEMALE STUDENT 1**
"But we've got class tomorrow, Mom! I can't go home. We've got class."

**MALE STUDENT 1**
The entire town was under martial law.

**FEMALE STUDENT 2**
There were bomb threats in the public schools.

**MALE STUDENT 1**
You weren't even allowed out on your porch after five o'clock.

**FEMALE STUDENT 2**
And we heard rumors that there were machine guns in some location near Brady Lake and that there were snipers . . .

**MALE STUDENT 1**
You had these helicopters buzzing all over town and National Guardsmen.

**FEMALE STUDENT 2**
. . . and that they had plans to poison the water supply of Kent.

**GUARDSMAN 1**
We stopped at a stop sign, and some students came out on their porch and started throwing stuff at us. And one of our fellas got out and pointed his rifle at the students and said,

**GUARDSMAN 2**

"Who wants to be first?"

**GUARDSMAN 1**

And they all dispersed and went back into the crowd. We went two blocks further and a grey-haired lady came out of her house with a plateful of cookies, and said

**OLD LADY**

"Here guys, here's some homemade cookies for you."

**GUARDSMAN 1**

So you could go a matter of a hundred feet from someone throwing rocks at you and calling you names and giving you the finger, to a nice old lady coming out and offering you cookies.

**FEMALE STUDENT 1**

I actually talked to a young guardsman, and he was very nonchalant, and said that he didn't really want to be here—it didn't mean a lot to him—he just had to come here because it was his job. But he pointed over to an older man, a small, ruggedly built older man who had a sidearm on his belt, and he said,

**GUARDSMAN 1**

"But with that guy over there, he really means business. He really gets into this."

**FEMALE STUDENT 1**

It seemed like it was "us versus them." In the paranoia of those precarious days, no one could see a peaceful resolution. Cambodia was crazy. Nixon was crazy. We thought the whole country was crazy. And, in turn, the governor and the police thought the students were crazy and uncontrollable.

**MALE STUDENT 1**

After the sun went down, I heard things happening, and then the helicopters began circling overhead. They have a certain frequency, a vibration that I can pick up in an instant from a great distance and right away.

**FEMALE STUDENT 3**

"Why don't you boys come up here and I can show you a good time!"

**GUARDSMAN 1**

At Tri-Towers we saw a woman standing naked against the window on the third floor.

**FEMALE STUDENT 3**

"Hey sailor, lookin' for a good time?"

**GUARDSMAN 1**

The room was dark behind her, and she had a light on her.

**FEMALE STUDENT 3**

Come on, take those uniforms off and get rid of those guns and I can show you a good time.

**GUARDSMAN 1**

We all laughed and hooted and our captain had to keep us in line.

**GUARDSMAN 2**

Sunday night, our captain said,

**GUARDSMAN 3**

"We're gonna look mean and green when we go down there. This is the big-time. We're gonna march in cadence."

**GUARDSMAN 2**

We had helicopters in the sky—a lot of radio traffic, a lot of bull-horns. A lot of confusion. I think at that time things sort of clicked. We all sort of said, "We're in the military now, and we gotta do what we're told to do." So we marched down and formed a perimeter around the ROTC building that was still smoldering in ashes. Then an officer came along and said to us,

**GUARDSMAN OFFICER**

"When the order is given to lock and load,"

**GUARDSMAN 2**

which in Army lingo means you take the ammunition out of your belt and put it into the weapon, and you lock it and you put it on 'safe'

**GUARDSMAN OFFICER**

"you are to lock and load, but you are not,"

**GUARDSMAN 2**

—and he made it very clear, almost to each of us there going down the line—

**GUARDSMAN OFFICER**

"you are not under any circumstances to fire unless you are given the order."

**GUARDSMAN 2**

We all checked; we all had a clip of eight rounds with us. We stood there for a while. It got dark.

**GUARDSMAN 1**

A lot of thoughts ran through my mind. If we're told to lock and load are we going to fire? Are we going to protect our lives? Are we going to run?

When the gas was laid down we started moving, and you could see the group that was there for just a party quickly disperse. They were out of there. It's at that point that I saw the students again let go with the rocks, and men waving their genitals at us, and women shouting obscenities. I was no virgin, and I was used to a lot of things, but I looked at this and I thought, "This gives me a whole different point of view on what's happening here."

**GUARDSMAN 2**

Then it got ugly. We had bayonets and they didn't. Things came flying out of the air. We were given the finger; we were yelled at. It was dark and there were a lot of high-intensity lights and helicopters were buzzing overhead. We came around a building and cornered a small group of students. We weren't chasing them. But it was the same group that had been mouthy and loud before, and now they were begging and pleading,

**MALE STUDENT 1**

"Don't hurt us, please; we didn't mean any harm."

**GUARDSMAN 2**

One of the females got hysterical and was yelling at the guy next to her,

**FEMALE STUDENT 1**

"I told you we shouldn't be here! Now look what's gonna happen to us!"

**GUARDSMAN 2**

We had masks on; we were anonymous. We had taken our nametags off our jackets. A fella down from me put a bayonet to a man's nose and said,

**GUARDSMAN 3**

"I know your face, but you don't know mine. If I ever see you again this is gonna go in your head."

**GUARDSMAN 2**

I think the man urinated himself right there on the spot. He had nowhere to go, nowhere to run. He was up against the wall with his hands up, and one of our guys ran his bayonet through his hand, pinned his hand right against the building. And another individual was slashed. The whole thing didn't take thirty seconds. It seemed like a flash in time. Then the guy who did the stabbing put his bayonet into the ground and pulled it out. He did this a couple of times, pointing at it to see if there was any blood still on it.

**GUARDSMAN 1**

We were told in no uncertain terms that we were not to run, we were not to fold, we were there to preserve the peace.

# SCENE FOUR: THE RALLY

Narrator

3 Male Students

**NARRATOR**

May 4. A clear, warm spring day, everything in blossom. It must have been after noon, when I watched a squad of National Guardsmen kneel, lock, and load in front of Satterfield. It never occurred to me, nor to anyone else I talked to, that the Guard carried live, steel jacketed ammunition. We did not think of ourselves as the enemy, dissidents but not enemy, believing the Guard to be on a peacekeeping mission, a civil action against an unarmed citizenry.

**MALE STUDENT 1**

I stood up at my abnormal psychology class at 11:00 on Monday morning and said I thought it was strange that the instructor was beginning to hold class without referencing the fact that there was a National Guard member standing at our doorway holding an M-1. I thought there should be some discussion, and, frankly, if there wasn't, I didn't think it was worth staying. So I urged everyone in class to come to the rally at noon, in defiance of the order not to gather. I mentioned the importance of our right to assemble. And I left that class with my abnormal psychology book in my hand and went to the rally.

**BLACK STUDENT 1**

I was aware of the rally, but at the same time, the Black United Students had encouraged us to stay away from the rally because they felt that if there were any kind of trouble, we would most likely be the first ones targeted. As far as we were concerned, the National Guardsmen were the police. And because we'd been subject to so much harassment and abuse by the police, I had no illusion that those guys had blanks or pellets in their rifles. We all assumed they had real bullets, and we would be the first ones to be shot.

**MALE STUDENT 2**

I stepped away from the crowd and I heard that they were reading the Riot Act. There were a lot of innocent people that had no idea the Riot Act was being read. Having been in the military, I had a grasp of military-think, and frankly didn't trust them. I knew the National Guard was edgy and had a reason to blow their cool. They were coming from at least two weeks of unwanted National Guard duty dealing with a truckers' strike in which there were real snipers using real bullets shooting from real guns from overpasses at independent truckers. This was a set-up for tragedy.

**BLACK STUDENT 1**

I saw people playing tennis on the courts behind Terrace Hall. So much of that day was just surreal. There were so many normal things going on.

**MALE STUDENT 1**

The army itself was the symbol of what everyone was angry about, and here was our own military kneeling and aiming rifles not just at protesters or rock throwers, but at a dormitory full of big glass windows filled with students. So you had these two groups facing off across the Commons, and by this time I think the anger on the part of the students was not Vietnam or Cambodia but "This is my home."

# SCENE FIVE: A VEIL IS RENT

4 Male Students
4 Female Students
2 Guardsmen

**FEMALE STUDENT 1**
Suddenly they turned and started firing.

**GUARDSMAN 1**
I didn't have my glasses on. I couldn't see very well through my gas mask.

**MALE STUDENT 1**
I saw people hitting the dirt, so I hit the dirt thinking, "Okay, okay."

**GUARDSMAN 2**
The men in front of me were aiming their rifles.

**FEMALE STUDENT 2**
The bullets whizzed past my ears.

**GUARDSMAN 1**
God, someone else is shooting. Did I miss an order?

**MALE STUDENT 2**
This is not what it sounds like on TV. This is not what bullets sound like on cartoons.

**GUARDSMAN 2**
I didn't know when to shoot, or what to shoot, or if I should shoot.

**MALE STUDENT 3**
It was a very different sound. A very different sound.

**FEMALE STUDENT 3**

It went on and on for what felt like eternity.

**GUARDSMAN 2**

Very quickly I heard the order, "Cease fire! Cease fire!"

**FEMALE STUDENT 2**

After the shooting, it got totally quiet. I just heard air hissing out of a tire—that sound, *bsssshhhoouu.*

**MALE STUDENT 1**

I looked around and it was as if time had stopped. Time had totally stopped. Now, subsequently, I've figured out what it was. When people die violently, a veil is rent and you're thrust into the next plane. And anyone who's tuned to the event feels this rush from a door opening. So the veil is rent, torn away. And any kind of evil thoughts that are there from humanity's beginning are available at this moment. And depending on how sensitive you are, you can hear it, feel it, or see it.

**FEMALE STUDENT 2**

And then there were screams.

**FEMALE STUDENT 3**

I didn't know if the whole campus had turned into a battleground. I didn't know just what was going to happen next. A couple of us thought, "They've already killed people. What's to say they're not gonna come in the building and start shooting?" We started looking around, trying to decide what to do. We were standing in the *Stater* office with floor-to-ceiling windows, and I said, "This is not the place to be." So we walked into the darkroom next door. I said, "If they shoot us here, they have to shoot through two cinderblock walls to get to us." There was an air vent, and I thought, "Oh my God, they'll throw tear gas in here. We need to close off that vent." So we got something and we taped over the vent. We made a bunker out of the darkroom.

**MALE STUDENT 1**

And then those guardsmen moved right past us. They moved within ten feet. I could've touched one of them. Everyone was frozen, and I could hear the stomping of their boots. And then I heard an *errrrrrrr,* like the gnashing of teeth, a demon kind of sound, because the veil was rent.

**MALE STUDENT 2**

And then the strangest thing happened. Maybe a thousand of us went to the other side of Taylor Hall where the Victory Bell was, and we formed a semicircle across from the Guard.

**MALE STUDENT 3**

Ten or twenty guys stripped to the waist and put X's on their chests, and their backs and foreheads. They were going to battle the guardsmen.

**MALE STUDENT 4**

After seeing our classmates shot, we got mad. We got really angry.

**MALE STUDENT 2**

We were all gone. It was freakville! There wasn't any rational thought now. It was a full-fledged riot.

**MALE STUDENT 1**

I mean, you felt like you were invincible, because you were so furious at what had happened.

**MALE STUDENT 2**

Our fear had disappeared, and we were ready to confront these people who had guns with nothing but our bodies.

**FEMALE STUDENT 1**

To this day, I am convinced that the Guard would have fired on more of us, and more of us would have been killed, if it had not been for Glenn Frank. He was a popular professor who taught geology in a large setting. He stood out there in a white, short-sleeved shirt with a pocket protector, with a grad student. They both had bullhorns and pleaded with us for calm and restraint. And gradually people began to listen. We sat down on the hill, and someone passed out popsicles. Bubblestick popsicles. Because in those years, people shared with each other. And when people had calmed down, he convinced us to go home. I am certain he saved a lot of people that day.

**GUARDSMAN 1**

Quite truthfully, had there not been our own soldiers in front of me, had I been in a different group—I can speak for myself, I would have fired.

**GUARDSMAN 2**

I wish you could put yourself in the mind-set of the guardsman pulling the trigger. For whatever reason, "God, someone else is shooting. Did I miss an order? I'm gonna do this. I've lost control. I've gained control. I have total control."

**GUARDSMAN 1**

I would have assumed that when others were firing, they were firing for a reason. I would have fired.

**GUARDSMAN 2**

To put yourself in the mind-set of the four or five days that led up to that. On both sides.

**FEMALE STUDENT 1**

One of our friends had ducked behind the same car as Allison Krause and had seen her die. Another friend of ours had ducked behind a tree that had a bullet hole chest-height when he came back out. I didn't know bullets could go through cars; that's how naive I was. Or trees. Lethally go through a tree. I tell you, to this day, May 4th is like Passover for me, because everybody I loved survived.

## FEMALE STUDENT 4

I had a grammar class that started at 1:10 in Satterfield. And I decided if I left Music and Speech and cut across the Commons, I might be able to get to class early enough to cram for my midterm exam. I walked across the Prentice Hall parking lot and saw tremendous amounts of blood.

The ambulances were already leaving, and there was blood everywhere. It looked like little rivulets of blood—puddles of blood—the whole parking lot. I couldn't figure out what was happening or why it had happened. There were students everywhere crying and holding hands and hugging each other. But still, I didn't know why, because I kept thinking of what my professor had said in speech class about the tear gas. I was convinced, for some crazy reason, that this was just tear gas. I had no clue where the blood was from. I had no clue where the ambulances were going, or why there were so many of them, why they were so loud and moving so fast, why people were crying so hard and hugging each other. So I kept walking. I didn't stop and talk to anyone. I just kept walking. I had a one-track mind. I had to get to Satterfield. It was almost like my body was being pulled. I had no control of it. I stopped nowhere, talked to no one, and just kept walking.

When I got to Satterfield, I sat down at my desk and began to cram for my test. At 1:10 I looked for my professor and my class, but they weren't there. No one was where they were supposed to be. I couldn't figure out what was going on and why the building was empty. Then somebody came up to me. I don't remember who it was, and they said, "You better go back to your dorm. There's been a problem on campus, you know. People have been shot. You better go back to your dorm."

So I walked all the way back to my dorm in Humphrey, which was far away from everything, and luckily, the girl who lived across the hall from me offered me a ride home to Cleveland. When we arrived, my mother was standing in the driveway crying, waiting for me, thinking I was one of the dead people at Kent. My neighbors were standing on their front lawns, and when they saw me get out of the car, everybody came over to touch me and said how glad they were to see me, and my mother just kept crying. But I didn't cry at all.

# SCENE SIX: INTENSIVE CARE

2 Male Students
1 Female Student
1 Young Kent Resident
1 Guardsman
1 Jr. High School Student
1 High School Student

*Headlines from newspapers on*
*May 5, 1970, called out*

Three are Dead, 12 Shot in Battle at Kent State

3 Dead, 15 Wounded in Rioting at KSU

Four Students Killed in Anti-Nixon Riot: Death of a Campus Bum

National Guardsmen Among Those Killed at Kent State

Kent Protestor Reported Killed

Three National Guardsmen Killed at Kent State

**YOUNG RESIDENT 1**

All day I watched my mother's back as she stood looking out the living room window. I didn't really understand what was going on. But I could tell from the line of her back and the tension in her neck that there was something very wrong.

**GUARDSMAN 1**

When my mother heard the news, she went bananas. She couldn't get through because they shut the phone lines down in Kent.

**YOUNG RESIDENT 1**

All the phone lines were down. There was no way that we could get through to the campus to find out where my two sisters and brother might be.

**GUARDSMAN 1**

So my mother and father loaded up the car to come out here. But I was able to get to a phone and call out, and I got ahold of Pittsburgh and said, "I'm fine; I'm alive; I can't talk," and hung up.

**JR. HIGH SCHOOL STUDENT**

A fellow student at Davey Junior High started screaming, because her mom and dad were on campus. School was closed immediately, and we were herded on buses.

**HIGH SCHOOL STUDENT**

They simply announced over the loudspeakers at the high school, "You will go home; you will not deter from your path. You will go straight home, and you will stay home."

**JR. HIGH SCHOOL STUDENT**

A very large man with a baseball bat came on board our bus to protect us, as everyone had the immediate fear of the unknown. We did not know then how many were shot, nor who was shot. The bus dropped us off on our corners and waited until every student was inside his house. We were all told to stay indoors.

**HIGH SCHOOL STUDENT**

I lived on West Main Street right at the Kent city limits, and when I got to my driveway there were two military vehicles parked at the top of the hill on Route 59, blockading the road. Nothing was coming into Kent. It was completely shut off.

**FEMALE STUDENT 1**

One family in our neighborhood packed everybody up in the car and left. They were terrified that great, vast hordes of radicals were going to come and invade—perhaps right on their front lawn.

**HIGH SCHOOL STUDENT**

We sat on our front porch and watched the pilgrimage—if that's what you could call it—all these people leaving the city, many of them walking. There was a look of astonishment on their faces—I don't know what the real word would be. But it was like a void in their eyes. I can't get over that hollow look in people's eyes.

**MALE STUDENT 1**

I had the radio in my car tuned to some news reports, as I was driving away from town. And the announcer said, "Okay, we'll be right back after some music and we'll tell you some more about what's happening at Kent State." And it was that song, "Everything is Beautiful," by Ray Stevens. I'd just come off campus with everything that I had seen. I saw a dead student in the street, I saw other people being carted away into ambulances, I saw the blood and the gore, and I'm sitting in the car listening to this song.

**MALE STUDENT 2**

I raced to the hospital, flashing my critical patient pass to the guards that were stationed on Route 59. My father was dying in the intensive care unit at Robinson Memorial Hospital on that day. He had checked in with gallstones a month earlier that turned out to be pancreatitis. My mother had been practically living at the hospital, sleeping on the couch outside the ICU, and going in every couple of hours to hold his hand. He had become nothing but skin and bones. We knew there was no way to save him. My father had been for the war, and my mom had been against it. But suddenly, it just didn't matter anymore with Dad dying and Mom at his side.

When I got there, my mom was already downstairs, and she told me he was gone. I asked her how it happened, and she said, "You won't believe it." She told me that when the ambulances arrived from the campus, she had heard the noise and commotion, and saw all the young people wheeled into the ICU. She said the doctors and nurses were crying, and one doctor went over and held up an x-ray to another and said, "Look where this bullet is lodged in this boy's spine. He's never going to walk again. In all my years of medicine, this is the most senseless thing I've ever seen." So my mom walked to the window and said, "Lord, Nick has had fifty-five good years. And all this time I've been praying that you would spare him. But how can I ask for that when these kids haven't even had twenty years? From now on, it's whatever you want." She turned around and went back into the ICU, and he was dead.

So my father died on May 4th, 1970. I've often thought about this and wondered if the student who was paralyzed, Dean Kahler, ever knew that my mother was there in the hospital, and how the doctors wept when they saw the bullet in his spine, and how those doctors and nurses were shocked and stunned and mortified at the waste—the senseless waste.

# SCENE SEVEN: REACTIONARY

Narrator
3 Male Students
2 Female Students
1 Faculty Member
1 BBC Producer
2 Kent Residents
1 Guardsman
1 Employer
1 Brother
1 Relative

### NARRATOR

Jeff Miller, who was a student of my friend Mike, was shot in the mouth at a distance of several hundred yards. That night I sat with Mike out in his yard, in the rain, as he drank and wept. I drank with him but couldn't find tears. I held him. He would not be consoled. As far as I know, Mike still isn't consoled. Something broke off inside him, like a city block sized chunk that shivers loose from one of those Antarctic ice caps and begins to wander the cold seas. Something in Mike broke loose and drifts inside him to this day.

### RESIDENT 1

On Tuesday morning my son and daughter went out to play with their friends in our neighbor's sandbox, because all the schools were closed. We were the only family connected to the university in our neighborhood, and everyone knew we were both against the war. About ten minutes later, my children came charging back through the door. My daughter was hysterical. She was holding onto her brother for dear life and screaming, "They threw stones at us, Mommy!" His face was covered in blood. Apparently, all the children in the sandbox who were usually their friends had collected stones and were waiting for them to arrive. I don't know what the parents had said to their children to make them think they could do this, but at that point, I thought these people were crazy. I decided my children weren't going anywhere without me. And everywhere they went that summer, even if it was just out into our little piece of garden, I went with them, or watched from the window.

**RESIDENT 2**

We started to get students turning up on our doorstep, pretty incoherent, bursting into tears, telling us how they had been kicked out of their homes. One student told us that his parents had screamed at him through the letterbox and said they never wanted to see him again.

**RESIDENT 1**

We were all a little reactionary. It was a really horrible summer. In fact, we didn't get any mail for nearly six weeks. We didn't even get bills. At one point that summer we were sitting near a window, and I said, "We've got to move away from the window." And so we went and sat in the corridor, because we thought some crazy neighbor would come and blow us away.

**RESIDENT 2**

I think what was the most upsetting was that you could almost understand why the shootings happened, because it was maybe people losing their temper under extreme, stressful situations.

**RESIDENT 1**

But we couldn't understand why all our neighbors had turned against us.

**RESIDENT 2**

How nobody spoke to us, how they crossed the street when we came toward them.

**RESIDENT 1**

How they could be so unreasonable, just because we were connected to the university.

**RESIDENT 2**

How they would phone us up and scream at us on the telephone.

**RESIDENT 1**

Even the little old neighbor we used to say hello to and shoveled snow from her driveway, because we thought she was too old to do it. These were the people that were turning on us.

**RESIDENT 2**

And so we kept to ourselves or to other faculty members. And we felt we were a sideshow that whole summer.

**FEMALE STUDENT 1**

I needed to get away. So I drove out to Virginia Kendall Park. It was a pretty day and I started walking on the trails in the woods. I was walking along and stepping on rocks, and I got this strange feeling that these were just like the ones I saw thrown. It was a weird sensation. But I couldn't touch the rocks, and I hated walking on them—they just felt bad. But I kept going and there was a ravine off to the side, and some fog and mist coming up from the water down in there. I caught it out of the corner of my eye and thought, "My God, why are they shooting tear gas here?" I knew this was stupid. It was mist, it was fog, and these were rocks. So I walked on a little bit farther, and a tree limb cracked behind me, and it sounded exactly like the bolt-action of a rifle. And I jumped back and yelled and hotfooted it out of there. It was like this whole thing was closing in on me.

**GUARDSMAN 1**

I went to my professor and told him that I had missed a test.

**FACULTY MEMBER**

"Well, why did you miss the test?"

**GUARDSMAN 1**

"Well, I was in the National Guard. I was on active duty."

**FACULTY MEMBER**

"Were you on this campus, too?"

**GUARDSMAN 1**

"Yeah."

**FACULTY MEMBER**

"You will never pass my course. You will never graduate from this university if I have anything to do with it. You have failed this course. And as far as I'm concerned, you shouldn't be permitted back on this campus."

**GUARDSMAN 1**

And he asked me to leave his office.

**MALE STUDENT 1**

I had a bad experience that summer when a group from the BBC came to interview me. They brought in a student who had been on campus, and tried to make some type of physical confrontation between me and this student. They put him real close to me to taunt me, and said,

**BBC PRODUCER**

"Why don't you do something now that you two are alone?"

**MALE STUDENT 1**

I stood up to leave the room, and he leaned back and said,

**MALE STUDENT 2**

"God, don't hit me, please!"

**MALE STUDENT 1**

I wasn't going to, but I got up and walked out of the room. The BBC man followed me out of the hotel,

**BBC PRODUCER**

"You signed a contract! You will never get a check from us."

**MALE STUDENT 1**

"That's the least of my worries."

**FEMALE STUDENT 2**

I applied for a summer job at a canning factory in Napoleon and I filled out the form and the woman read where it said I was going to Kent State . . .

**EMPLOYER**

"Are you a Communist?"

**FEMALE STUDENT 2**

To me it was an absurd question but she was asking me very seriously. When I got back to school that fall I found out a whole lot of people were asked if they were Communists.

**MALE STUDENT 1**

At a family reunion one of my relatives was really angry with me because she thought I went to Ohio State, and there'd been some disturbances at Ohio State. So I just listened. And then my helpful brother came up and said,

**BROTHER**

"Oh, he doesn't go to Ohio State. He goes to Kent State."

**RELATIVE**

"If I had been there I would have shot them all."

**MALE STUDENT 3**

So I took a bus to Columbus to arrest Governor Rhodes for criminal misconduct. I knew it was kind of nuts. People don't usually do those kind of things. But I went into his office, and this lady said, "May I help you?" And I said, "I'm here to make a citizen's arrest of

Governor Rhodes for criminal misconduct in regard to the Kent State shootings of two days ago." And she gave me this look that I'm not sure I could ever put into words. It's a wonder she didn't have a heart attack. I felt guilty about it, really, because people are creatures of habit, and I'm sure she never anticipated this would be a part of her daily activity.

So this gentleman with a suit came out. I think he was the chief of security. And he explained to me that you can only make a citizen's arrest if you observe a felony. He said even though there are people who would question Governor Rhodes' handling or mishandling of this incident, depending on their perspective, this wasn't that kind of situation. He said, "For example, you can't go and make a citizen's arrest of President Nixon and accuse him of being a war criminal. Our society just isn't set up for that, even though people of an idealistic bent might think it is." But he said he really respected the fact that I cared enough to put myself out there. Most people wouldn't. So that was kind of the thrust of the whole conversation. And he was the most cordial, likeable person you'd ever want to meet. He had really good people skills. We talked for a long time. Maybe an hour or so. And when we had finished, he said, "You understand, now, why you can't make a citizen's arrest of the governor?" And I said, "I do," and thanked him for talking with me, and left, feeling somehow that I had intruded on his time.

### RESIDENT 1

While most of us were trying to put our lives back together, a notice went around for people to join a choral presentation of The Cherubini Requiem. Some members of the Cleveland Orchestra came down to the United Church of Christ in Kent and joined with some local folks. I don't have a very good voice, but I enjoy choral singing a lot. I'd been involved in choruses before in college. But my neighbor has an excellent voice. And so she and I agreed to go together, and she allowed me to stand next to her, so I could be sure to hit the right notes. We went to all of the rehearsals together, and I have such a vivid memory of that performance. We had to unbuckle the pews to make room for everyone. We filled up all the pews and all the balcony. And I have never had such a high, I think, in doing anything else. And the most exhilarating part of it was at the end, where it trails off to a pianissimo—it became very quiet.

And nobody applauded. There was complete silence in the church. And then, gradually, people began to stand up, while we just stood there. And I felt like the whole inside of me was screaming.

# SCENE EIGHT:
## GETTING IN THE WAY OF BULLETS

2 Male Students
1 Female Student
1 Faculty Member
1 Mom
3 Fbi Agents
2 Police Officers
1 Prosecutor
1 Sheriff
1 Attorney General
1 BBC Producer
2 Residents
1 Guardsman


**MALE STUDENT 1**

There was a knock on the door. Two guys in suits who said they were FBI agents wanted to interview Matthew Erwin. And my mom said,

**MOM**

"I think you're looking for the wrong guy. I think you want Mike Erwin."

**MALE STUDENT 1**

And one of the agents said,

**FBI AGENT 1**

"Ma'am, we want Matthew Erwin."

**MOM**

"Are you sure you want Matthew, because Mike is my eldest son and I think that's who you want to talk to."

**MALE STUDENT 1**

And the guy got real snippy with her and said,

**FBI AGENT 1**

"Lady, we want to talk to Matthew Erwin."

**MALE STUDENT 1**

Well, Matt was my youngest brother. He was six years old, and he'd been particularly bratty that day. So my mom grabbed him and pushed him out the door with the FBI agents and slammed the door. A couple seconds later, we heard a knock.

**FBI AGENT 1**

"Ma'am, this isn't who we want to talk to."

**MOM**

"You asked to speak with Matthew Erwin, you'll speak with Matthew Erwin!"

**MALE STUDENT 1**

You like to think this is America, and people don't disappear. But I didn't know what would have happened if I had said I wouldn't go with them. So I went, and they showed me picture after picture after picture. And after the first ten minutes, I realized they had no intention of figuring out what had happened.

**FEMALE STUDENT 1**

I think their way of investigating was a kind of "Who were you with?" syndrome. They'd interview somebody in Cleveland and say,

**FBI AGENT 2**

"Except for anyone you know in Cleveland, who were you with?"

**FEMALE STUDENT 1**

"Well, I was with Art from Philadelphia."

**MALE STUDENT 1**

They just wanted to identify people, and they wanted to pin things on people.

**FEMALE STUDENT 1**

And so they were at his doorstep. And the last statement the FBI agent would make was,

**FBI AGENT 2**

"Except for anyone you know in Cleveland, who were you with?"

**MALE STUDENT 2**

"I was with my roommate Steve from Connecticut."

**MALE STUDENT 1**

And it became real apparent that no one in a position of authority gave a hoot about what had really happened and the underlying causes. They just wanted to find people to blame it on.

**FEMALE STUDENT 1**

And the next day, they were at his door! So that's how they pyramided the investigation.

**MALE STUDENT 1**

I couldn't drive through my hometown without the local police stopping me:

**POLICE OFFICER 1**

"Uh, your tail light is out—oh, it looks fine now—well, it was out when I stopped you."

**MALE STUDENT 1**

One night, I was driving with my best friend, who worked for the police department and did towing for them. Well, the policeman looked down and saw that he was in the car and said,

**POLICE OFFICER 2**

"You know you really need to pick your friends better."

**FACULTY MEMBER**

We had people knocking on our door, wanting to rent our garage, supposedly because they'd been thrown out of their apartments. They looked more hippie than any hippie you ever saw. They had these awful sort of "ban the bomb"–type nuclear disarmament symbols, with really ugly shirts and things. I felt sure they were definitely FBI, and I wouldn't let them in. One of the guys tried to get in the door, like,

**FBI HIPPIE**

"Hey man,"

**FACULTY MEMBER**

acting really friendly with me, like he was just one of my group of people. It was really bizarre. Everyone was so caught up with the mania. I mean, he could have planted a bug—who knows what he could have done. We felt we were being watched and dissected, and everyone was trying to find out about some conspiracy.

**MALE STUDENT 1**

Of course, because I had been so cooperative with the investigation, when subpoenas went out for the Grand Jury, I got one. My father went over to the Portage County Courthouse with me. I'd gotten a haircut and was wearing a sports coat and tie to play the game. One of the court officials put us in the waiting room. And after a while, I needed to use the facilities. So I asked this guy who was right outside the door if I could use the bathroom. And as loud as he could he hollered,

**POLICE OFFICER 1**

"What's the matter, hippie, you need to take a bath? Hey! Here's one that needs to take a bath!"

**MALE STUDENT 1**

I kept having this naive hope that people really wanted to find out what happened. But when I got into the Grand Jury room itself and got up on the stand, I was asked questions for about fifteen minutes or so, and then I was shown where I was on the map and all that stuff. But those questions were just the preliminaries. I didn't realize they could turn the jury loose on the witness. There were probably half a dozen people who actually stood up and yelled at me and lectured me about what I should have done and how unpatriotic I was.

**MALE STUDENT 2**

So I got a phone call on a Friday night. A man identified himself as a detective from the Portage County Sheriff.

**SHERIFF**

"I can't tell you why I'm calling you. But if you would like to take a guess, I can tell you yes or no."

**MALE STUDENT 2**

"I've been indicted."

**SHERIFF**

"Yes."

**MALE STUDENT 2**

The special prosecutor said,

**PROSECUTOR**

"They should've shot all the troublemakers."

**MALE STUDENT 2**

And this is the prosecutor for a supposedly unbiased and objective Grand Jury. The Attorney General said,

**ATTORNEY GENERAL**

"Probably no guardsmen would be indicted."

## MALE STUDENT 2

So they were setting the stage for a whitewash. And the university was admonished for allowing the Jefferson Airplane to play at Homecoming, for students going barefoot and professors not saluting the flag. I mean, it was absolutely absurd. And in the Grand Jury report, they never mentioned four students were killed. They exonerated the National Guard, and they indicted twenty-five students and faculty, including two of the wounded students. The morbid joke was that they were guilty of getting in the way of bullets.

# SCENE NINE: VIGIL

Narrator
5 Male Students
5 Female Students
1 Guardsman
2 Alumni

**NARRATOR**

At sunset on May 4th, I left Kent and headed back to Illinois. The National Guard had sealed off Kent. I drove up to one of the checkpoints across Route 43, just south of the 261 intersection. A young, ill at ease guardsman checked my driver's license, took down the information on a clipboard, and set aside the barricade. I was a shaggy bearded fella back then, and as my wife and I drove through, the National Guard officer, a lieutenant, gave us the finger, smacking his elbow in his cupped hand for emphasis. I am his other and he is mine. The Greek root of the word compassion means to feel the viscera of the other. If there is to be peace, I must feel his viscera. He must feel mine. I don't know of another way.

**MALE STUDENT 1**

We were really pissed! But we didn't know what to do with that anger. And there wasn't anybody in those days to counsel us. The guys coming home from Vietnam—nobody counseled them. So they became murderers and drug addicts and killed themselves in cars. You're a man! Take it like a man! Well, that's just crap. Nobody came out of the woodwork to help us. Nobody.

**MALE STUDENT 2**

So I got indicted in the "Kent 25," and this was almost as traumatic for me as the May 4th tragedy was itself . . .

**GUARDSMAN 1**

We didn't really ever talk about it, hardly even among our friends.

**MALE STUDENT 2**

. . . 'cause I was a twenty-one-year-old man, and suddenly, the lights of repression were shining on me.

**GUARDSMAN 1**

And to this day it's amazing to me that in all of the company of Guards—and there's forty or fifty people in a company—no one in my company knew anyone involved in that shooting.

**MALE STUDENT 3**

(*same actor from scene one napalm story*)
God knows why I was indicted, except that my dog napalming demonstration put the focus on me. Otherwise, I was one of two thousand people out there on the Commons that day.

**GUARDSMAN 1**

So the people that were involved really clammed up, and no one's ever talked to us about it.

**FEMALE STUDENT 1**

Not only did 58,000 Americans die in Vietnam, but *we* killed two million of *them*. It's never mentioned really.

**FEMALE STUDENT 2**

I think a whole lot of people knew what was happening.

**FEMALE STUDENT 1**

Two million. We visited forty times as many deaths upon the Vietnamese and Cambodians as they visited upon us.

**FEMALE STUDENT 2**

And they were going to make an example out of Kent.

**MALE STUDENT 2**

And where better than a middle-class, basically white school, with kids who weren't too rich, where the parents couldn't possibly be a threat to the government.

**MALE STUDENT 3**

And that we had enough savvy, as kids, to have compassion for the Vietnamese. I mean, we could have been drinking beer at a frat party instead. We didn't have to protest, right?

**FEMALE STUDENT 2**

It was different than Jackson State. Look at the small amount of publicity they got, because they were a small, black, Southern institution. Whereas we were a large, white, middle-class, midwestern institution that was fairly well-known. So it was like the ideal place for the government to make an example of the student protest and antiwar movement: "We're going to put these kids down, literally! And they're never going to get back up again! And this antiwar movement is going to be ended once and for all!" It makes so much sense to me.

**MALE STUDENT 4**

I don't consider myself to be very spiritual.

**FEMALE STUDENT 3**

Sometimes I feel over the years that my spirit went back toward the seed and not toward the flower.

**MALE STUDENT 4**

But when I look at films or pictures of the ROTC building burning and collapsing, it's as if it were a part of hell, a portal. And all that is associated with hell manifested itself there and fed upon the souls of the Guard, and upon the souls of the students, and of the townspeople and officials.

**FEMALE STUDENT 3**

So my life has been a stand ever since.

**MALE STUDENT 4**

I just kept pretty much to myself and left school and pretty much dropped out of society and went and lived in the mountains of Colorado.

**FEMALE STUDENT 3**

It's kind of sent me on a search.

**MALE STUDENT 4**

I couldn't talk about it.

**FEMALE STUDENT 3**

You know, kind of searching for truth and justice and freedom, and those other sixties values.

**MALE STUDENT 5**

It wasn't until years after that I ever really mentioned to anybody that I had thrown a rock that day. And not that I hadn't already started on my way to becoming an alcoholic, but I did nothing but drink for ten years.

**FEMALE STUDENT 3**

Kent State was not just Kent State. It was a symbol for everything, and it was indicative of everything at that time. And, as they've said, that was the day the war came home.

**ALUMNUS 1**

I've come back to so many of the May 4th commemorations, and it's pretty strange . . .

**ALUMNUS 2**

At first, the town seemed oddly familiar, although strange too.

**ALUMNUS 1**

I rolled in last night and it's like meeting an old girlfriend you haven't seen for a while.

**ALUMNUS 2**

I'm never able to stop talking about it. I was on campus for the thirtieth anniversary, and there were a couple of people that I'm sure I hadn't seen since the morning of May 4th.

**ALUMNUS 1**

I saw a trio of cute female students who were laughing and planning to get into trouble, apparently.

**ALUMNUS 2**

And it was wild to see so many grown men—lots of gray beards around—just openly weeping over what we had gone through.

**ALUMNUS 1**

They were young and they whirred out of the parking lot with no need of morbid ceremonies for the famous dead.

**ALUMNUS 2**

And you can tell talking to some of these people that they've held it in and have never let it out before.

**ALUMNUS 1**

Those kids are the future and they represent life. I wonder what, if anything, May 4th means to them.

**FEMALE STUDENT 4**

You have to tell the truth. And I'm not sure that the truth has been told—that there were repressive elements, that there were radical students, that there were confused eighteen-year-olds. There were lots of truths.

**FEMALE STUDENT 5**

Last time I came to the candlelight vigil, I stood next to the marker where Jeffrey Miller's body had lain, and his parents stood there inside that marker. They were so dignified. It struck me that they were getting older and their son would always be nineteen.

**MALE STUDENT 1**

*(\*same actor as Male student 1 in scene five)*

So, what do we have now? We have this past that's painful and we have this future that could be bright. My job—and this is the only job I have—is to make sure that the future is bright, that optimism prevails!

My whole existence now is about helping people through the veil, because I know it exists. And when I'm present at people's deaths, I sit at their beds and whisper instructions on how to get through the veil. Because everybody dies. No one escapes that one. No one. But we have no counselors; we have no philosophers; we have nobody on this side in America telling us, "Wow, it's not just about being twenty or thirty, your youth. It's about living and getting older." And when you're older, supposedly, having wisdom. So the goal is a positive, spiraling motion. Forward. Forward. Forward.

**NARRATOR**

Forty years later, spring comes again. I live on the other side of the Cuyahoga River in a small house on a dead end street. I haven't gotten very far. This afternoon, my daughter Megan cut the grass. I weeded the flowerbed. Maintenance. Provisional orders. A wooden fence marks where our property ends and the neighbor's begins. Everything is in its place.

I offer not a consolation but an understanding. I know they are not the same. The Buddhists tell us we all have three hearts, linked one to the other, like Christmas lights in a series. First is the heart of compassion, then the heart of love, finally the heart of wisdom. They open in that order, no other. Compassion, that heart once opened, prompts the opening of the heart of love and that, in turn, signals the opening of the heart of wisdom. What is not love is fear. Meet your rage on the threshing floor of the first heart. No other way. That simple. Feel that. Start there.

Tomorrow, I'll find my way up to the Commons to hear the ringing of the bell to commemorate the dead and the wounded. The bell is a voice. Everything in Kent is in blossom. And every blossom is listening.

# AFTERWORD

*Judith Royer and Doris Baizley*

*May 4th Voices* is full of surprising discoveries. The wife of a dying man prays for a wounded Kent State student just brought into the same intensive care unit as her husband . . . a high school teacher steps in front of a young antiwar student being pelted with little pebbles from a crowd of enraged bigger kids . . . a man speaks, for the first time, about having thrown a rock at a National Guardsman that fateful day and how he believes it was part of what began his ten years of drinking. These remembered moments are so vivid, so layered with meaning, metaphor, action and revelation—it is hard to imagine any playwright could invent a more powerful dramatization of the events that occurred before, during, and continued long after the Kent State shootings than we have in these personal verbatim accounts.

Whatever we thought we knew about Kent State from the news or history books, there will be something in this play that will be a discovery for everyone. Whether it's called "verbatim theatre," "dramatized narrative," "theatre of testimony," or just plain "documentary," *May 4th Voices* puts on stage the experiences of people whose stories might never be heard, or at best will be filed away in university library archives, and on that stage turns them into art. This experience of speaking our stories takes us back to the very essence of theatre as a shared community event.

In recent years, theatre artists and audiences have rediscovered this essential theatrical element as demonstrated in the work of Anna Deveare Smith, the late Jo Carson, Moisés Kaufman and the Tectonic Theater Project, and Cornerstone Theatre, to name only a few. With *May 4th Voices,* we welcome a company of vital new contributors to the field.

*May 4th Voices* is especially significant for its home site value. The ongoing Kent State Shootings Oral History Project, begun in 1990 by Sandra Perlman Halem and now housed in the Kent State University Libraries' Department of Special Collections and Archives, is important for preserving documentation of this historical event from many personal, conflicting, official, and unofficial points of view. Now, with

David Hassler's play and Katherine Burke's collaborative direction, these accounts can be presented in performance on-site, in the university and city where the events occurred, and where audiences may include original participants, their families, and a next generation of Kent citizens, providing for all the opportunity for better understanding of a common past.

However, this play also extends beyond local significance. As FEMALE STUDENT 3 says (in Scene 9, "Vigil"): "Kent State was not just Kent State. It was a symbol for everything. . . . as they've said, that was the day the war came home." For those of us who remember the Vietnam War, every voice in this play resonates with our own experiences and takes us back to reflect on and reexamine that time. Of even more importance, however, these voices bring the conflict alive in a present-tense, dramatic immediacy. The national crisis of 1970 is suddenly live and in front of us as a parallel to our present-day crises and conflicts. It is even possible that performing the play will help answer ALUMNUS 1's question for some of us: "These kids are the future. They represent life. I wonder, what, if anything, May 4th means to them?"

For artists/educators, the play offers yet another benefit. It is a well thought through and skillfully executed model for developing cross-disciplinary "culture studies" teaching projects. For those who work in universities, it provides an excellent example of how to develop a learning experience that can connect theatre departments with many other disciplines. With the economic pressure on most professional and academic theatres, this kind of play-making presents a creative outlet for writers and actors, fills a need for communities who want their stories told, and builds a future audience of truly engaged theatergoers.

On a personal note, for the two authors of this Afterword who remember well the Kent State shootings, the last scene, "Vigil: Legacy of Trauma," provided them with a new, very moving and insightful discovery about the events. It revealed a PTSD-type of response suffered by so many of the participants, which has been largely ignored in most studies about May 4th and which is given voice so personally and powerfully in this play.

As the narrator tells us in the final speech of the play, *May 4th Voices* offers "not a consolation, but an understanding."